Read Something Else

READ SOMETHING ELSE

Collected & Dubious
Wit & Wisdom of

Lemony Snicket

HARPER
An Imprint of HarperCollinsPublishers

www.harpercollinschildrens.com
Library of Congress Control Number: 2018954193
ISBN 978-0-06-285421-6
Book design by Alison Donalty & Alice Wang

19 20 21 22 23 PC/LSCC 10 9 8 7 6 5 4 3 2 1
❖ First Edition

All the SECRETS of the WORLD are contained in BOOKS

Introduction

All the secrets of the world are contained in books—read at your own risk.

*

No one has ever said, "Please let me stay up a little later—I am reading a really good book's introduction."

*

If a book is the beginning of a conversation between the author and the reader, then the first few pages are just the author clearing his throat.

*

Ahem, ahem, ahem.

*

A reader once remarked to me, "Mr. Snicket, instead of collecting your own thoughts into a book, why don't you gather what other people have—wait, why are you writing this down?"

*

Taking a few sentences from a book and putting them by themselves is like removing a few sheep from a meadow. The sheep might get lonely, but you might find them delicious.

*

When you read a sentence you love, you might pause for a moment to think about it, leaving your finger right there in the book so you do not lose your place. It is very important to retrieve your finger when you are done.

*

Reading very short things is like opening a box of candied violets. You promise yourself you will only eat one, but before you know it, the whole day is gone and an angry mob is driving you out of town.

*

Some books should be read straight through, a phrase which here means "from the first page to the last," and some books can be read by skipping around, a phrase which here means "romping around outside instead of reading."

*

The best books are like complicated surgery— first you can't get your head out of them, and then you can't get them out of your head.

*

The end of a book's introduction is like the end of childhood. There is still so much ahead to disappoint you.

*

Most people skip a book's introduction, so it's a good place to hide secrets.

Just because something is typed—whether it is typed on a business card or typed in a newspaper or book—this does not mean that it is true.

The sad truth

is that the

truth is sad.

No matter
who you are,
no matter
where you live, and
no matter
how many people
are chasing you,
what you don't read
is often as important as
what you do read.

IF EVERYONE FOUGHT
FIRE WITH FIRE,
THE ENTIRE WORLD
WOULD GO UP
IN SMOKE.

THE BAD BEGINNING

One of the world's tiresome questions is what object one would bring to a desert island, because people always answer "a deck of cards" or *"Anna Karenina"* when the obvious answer is "a well-equipped boat and a crew to sail me off the island and back home where I can play all the card games and read all the Russian novels I want."

JUST ABOUT
EVERYTHING IN THIS
WORLD IS EASIER
SAID THAN DONE, WITH
THE EXCEPTION OF

"systematically assisting Sisyphus's
stealthy, cyst-susceptible sister,"

WHICH IS EASIER DONE
THAN SAID.

Having an aura of menace is like having a pet weasel, because you rarely meet someone who has one, and when you do it makes you want to hide under the coffee table.

A fluffy poached egg is a good breakfast, and a good breakfast is better than a bad one, like a good book is better than having your toe chopped off.

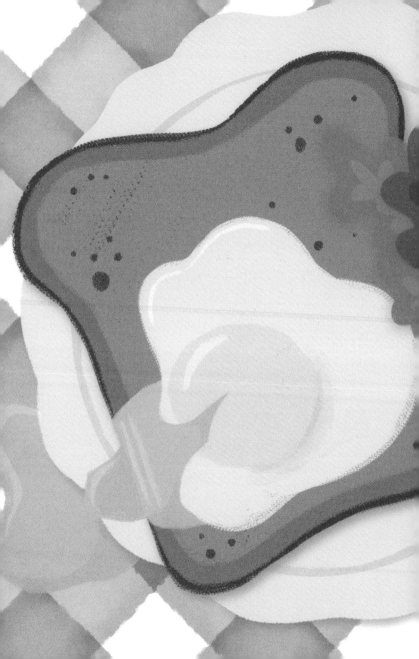

A good friend tells you
that the meal was delicious.
A great friend
does the dishes.

The Carnivorous Carnival

Lemony Snicket

Should you read

in the morning,

the afternoon,

or in the middle of the night?

Yes.

Fate is like a strange, unpopular restaurant, filled with odd waiters who bring you things you never asked for and don't always like.

Somewhere in the world is an acorn waiting to grow into a tree waiting to be chopped down to be made into paper waiting for an author to write something that someone might appreciate, such as *"Thank you, acorn."*

NORMALLY IT IS NOT POLITE TO GO INTO SOMEBODY'S ROOM WITHOUT KNOCKING, BUT YOU —CAN— MAKE AN EXCEPTION IF THE PERSON IS DEAD, OR PRETENDING TO BE DEAD

Don't repeat yourself.
It's not only repetitive,
it's redundant,
and people have
heard it before.

*Don't repeat yourself.
It's not only repetitive,
it's redundant,
and people have
heard it before.*

Tears are curious things,
for like earthquakes
or puppet shows they can occur
at any time, without any warning
and without any good reason.

You don't spend your life
hanging around books
without learning a thing
or two.

There is no point in delaying crying.
Sadness is like having a vicious
alligator around.
You can ignore it for only so long before
it begins devouring things and you
have to pay attention.

The trouble with doing something suspicious for a living is that your coworkers will likely be suspicious, too, and you will find yourself entangled in a web of suspicion, even during your lunch hour.

When trouble strikes,
head to the library.
You will either be able to
solve the problem,
or simply have something
to read as the world
crashes down around you.

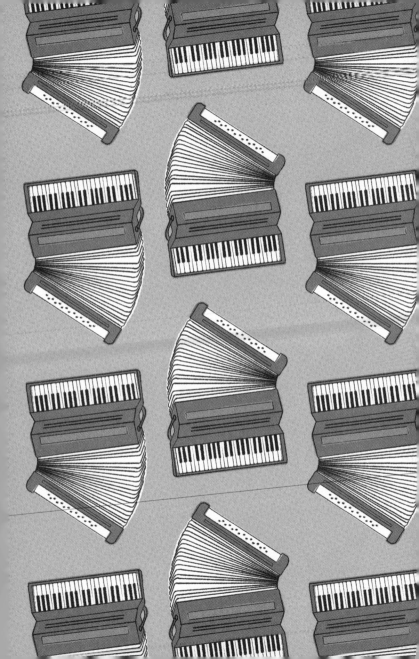

It is most likely that
I will die next to a pile of books
I was meaning to read.

A family is like a fire exit. If it doesn't work properly,
there's no reason to run toward it.

One of the remarkable things about **LOVE** is that, despite very irritating people writing poems and songs about how pleasant it is, it really is quite pleasant.

"NO NEWS IS

"No news is good news" simply means that if you don't hear from someone, everything is probably fine, and you can see at once why this expression makes such little sense, because everything being fine is only one of many, many reasons

why someone may contact you. Perha they are tied up. May they are surrounded fierce weasels, or haps they are wedg tightly between t refrigerators and not get themselves The expression mi well be changed

"No news is bad news,

GOOD NEWS."

---

cept that people may
t be able to contact
u because they have
t been crowned king
are competing in
gymnastics tourna-
nt. The point is that
re is no way to know
y someone has not
tacted you, until
y contact you and
lain themselves. For
s reason, the sensible

expression would be

"No news is no news,"

except that it is so ob-
vious it is hardly an ex-
pression at all.

Villainy can win against
one library,
but not against an organization
of readers.

———————

It's an important skill to know
when not to say anything.
It's not a skill that came naturally to me then,
nor does it come naturally now,
nor do I expect it to come naturally to me
until I am dead, when I will be
very, very good at it.

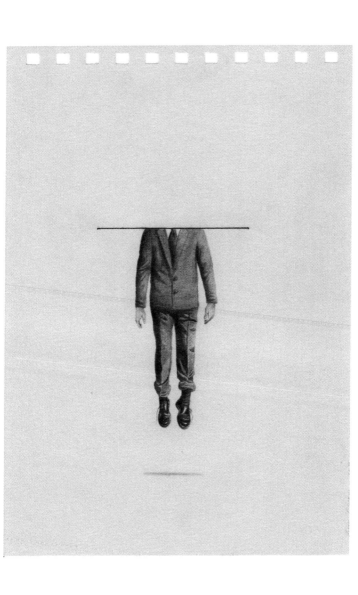

People aren't either
wicked or noble.
They're like chef's salads, with
good things and bad things
chopped and mixed
together in a vinaigrette
of confusion and conflict.

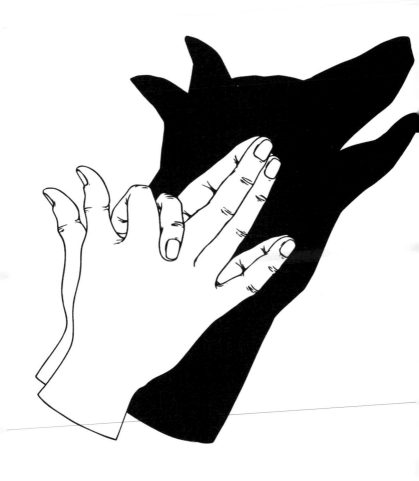

Nobody is too old to be afraid of the dark. The dark is a terrifying place, because in the dark one cannot tell if that creaking sound is just a branch in the wind or the claw of a half-dog, half-eagle creature that is hungry for human flesh.

*NOTHING FIRMS UP
A FRIENDSHIP
LIKE A GOOD-NATURED
ARGUMENT.*

A SERIES OF UNFORTUNATE EVENTS

LEMONY SNICKET

THE REPTILE ROOM

Strange as it may seem, I still hope for the best, even though the best, like an interesting piece of mail, so rarely arrives, and even when it does it can be lost so easily.

A library is like an island in the middle of
a vast sea of ignorance,
particularly if the library is very tall and
the surrounding area has been flooded.

Miracles are like pimples, because once you start looking for them you find more than you ever dreamed you'd see.

It is one of life's bitterest truths that bedtime so often arrives just when things are really getting interesting.

Assumptions are dangerous things to make,

and like all dangerous things to make—

bombs, for instance, or strawberry shortcake—

if you make even the tiniest mistake you can find

yourself in terrible trouble.

One of the most
troublesome things in life
is that what you
do or do not want
has very little to do with what
does or does not happen.

Those unable to catalog the past

are doomed to repeat it.

DO THE SCARY THING FIRST,

AND GET SCARED LATER.

TRY NOT TO GET CRUMBS ON THE FLOOR.

There's nothing wrong
with occasionally staring
out the window and
thinking nonsense,
as long as the
nonsense is yours.

The Wide Window

Lemony Snicket

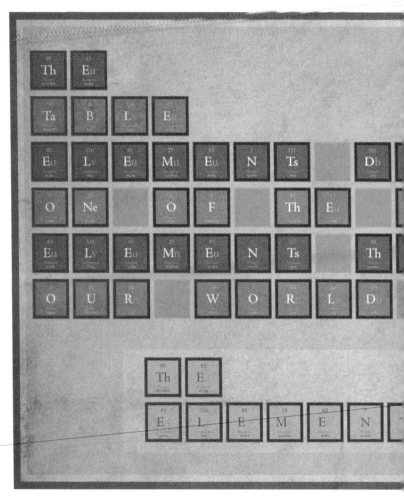

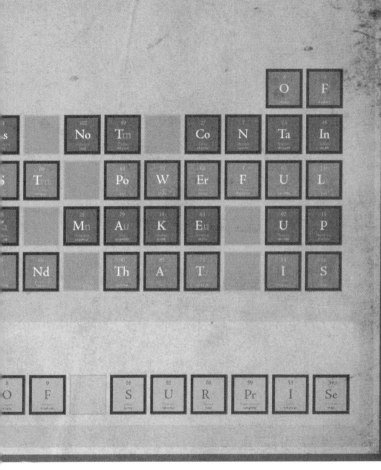

Everyone should be able to do

one card trick,

tell two jokes, and

recite three poems,

in case they are ever trapped in an elevator.

We are all told to ignore bullies.

It's something they teach you,

and they can teach you anything.

It doesn't mean you learn it.

It doesn't mean you believe it.

One should never ignore bullies.

One should stop them.

Ringing someone up in the morning

is like wringing their neck at night.

You'd best have a very good reason.

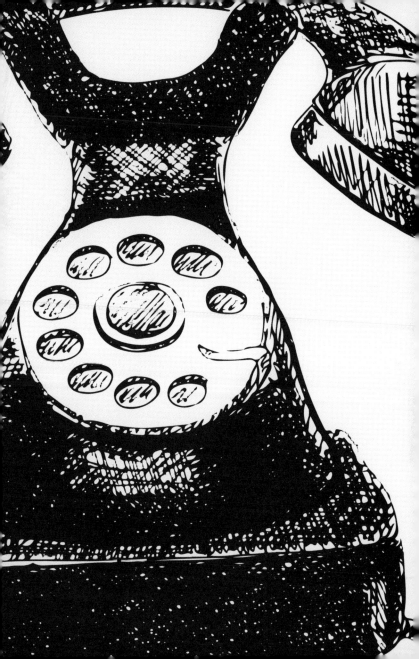

It is good to brush your teeth when you are angry, because you brush harder and do a better job.

You might be afraid of

the dark,

but the dark is

not afraid of you.

That's why

the dark is

always close by.

You cannot wait for an untroubled world to have an untroubled moment. The terrible phone call, the rainstorm, the sinister knock on the door—they will all come. Soon enough arrive the treacherous villain and the unfair trial and the smoke and the flames of the suspicious fires to burn everything away. In the meantime, it is best to grab what wonderful moments you find lying around.

Oftentimes, when people
are miserable,
they will still want
to make other people
miserable, too.
But it never helps.

The Ersatz Elevator

Lemony Snicket

THE BEST WAY TO
KEEP A SECRET
S TO TELL IT TO EVERYONE
YOU KNOW, BUT
PRETEND YOU ARE
KIDDING.

The quoting of an aphorism,

like the angry barking of a dog or the smell of

overcooked broccoli, rarely indicates

that something helpful is about to happen.

If an optimist had his left arm chewed off by an alligator, he might say, in a pleasant and hopeful voice, "Well, this isn't too bad. I don't have my left arm anymore, but at least nobody will ever ask me whether I am right-handed or left-handed," but most of us would say something more along the lines of "Aaaaah! My arm! My arm!"

*You cannot have a really
terrific library without at least one
terrific librarian,
the way you cannot have a really
terrific bedroom unless you can
lock the door.*

It is always cruel to laugh at people, of course, although sometimes if they are wearing an ugly hat it is hard to control yourself.

Shyness is a curious thing, because, like quicksand, it can strike people any time, and also, like quicksand, it makes its victims look down.

There is a popular game in which one person says something to another, and that person says it to another, and so on and so on, and all the while the message is getting more and more garbled until it is nonsense. The game is called "living in the world" and it has been played for thousands of years.

It is very difficult to make one's way in this world without being wicked at one time or another, when the world's way is so wicked to begin with.

Reading is one form of escape.

Running for your life

is another.

The Austere Academy

Lemony Snicket

In my experience,
well-read people are
less likely to be evil.

Taking one's chances is like taking
a bath, because sometimes you end up
feeling comfortable and warm, and
sometimes there is something terrible
lurking around that you cannot see until
it is too late and you can do nothing else
but scream and cling to a plastic duck.

It is almost as if happiness is an acquired taste,
like coconut cordial or ceviche, to which you can
eventually become accustomed,
but despair is something surprising each time
you encounter it.

SHOWING UP EARLY IS ONE OF THE SIGNS OF A NOBLE PERSON.

*ALL CANNOT BE LOST
WHEN THERE IS STILL SO MUCH
BEING FOUND.*

As I'm sure you know,
the key to good eavesdropping
is not getting caught.

If you are allergic to a thing, it is best not to put that thing in your mouth, particularly if the thing is cats.

THE SEA
IS NOTHING BUT
A LIBRARY OF
ALL THE TEARS
IN HISTORY.

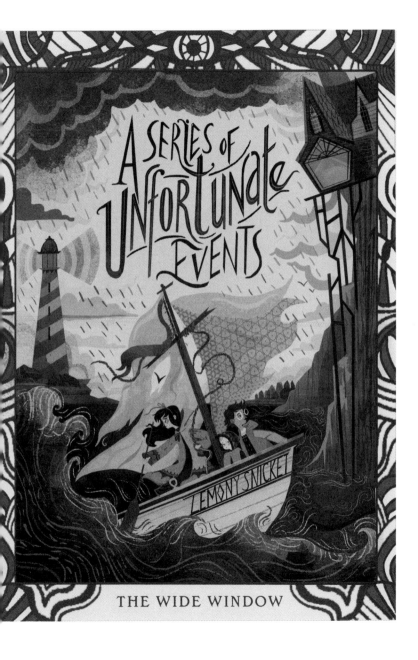

A SERIES OF UNFORTUNATE EVENTS

LEMONY SNICKET

THE WIDE WINDOW

If we wait until

we are ready,

we'll be waiting

for the rest of

our lives.

Some books are like trapdoors, because you go through them once and leave them behind, and some are like fishnets, because they provide you with sustenance for years.

Love can change
a person the way
a parent can change
a baby—awkwardly,
and often with a great
deal of mess.

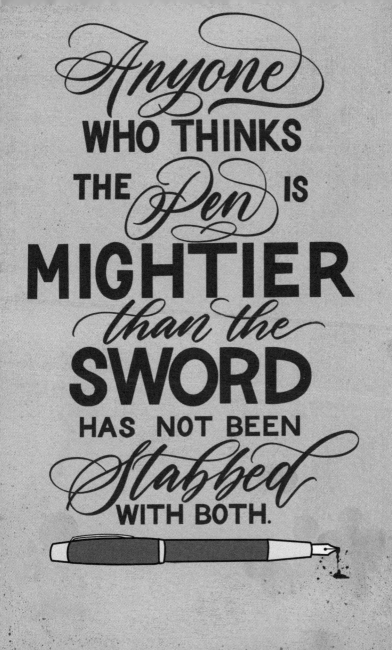

They say in every library there is a single book that can answer the question that burns like a fire in the mind.

If writers wrote as carelessly

as some people talk, then

adhasdh asdglaseuyt[bn[pasdlgkhasdfasdf.

Friends are like napkins.
Keep a good stack handy
for messy days.

The moral of

"Snow White" is

"Never eat apples."

The End

Lemony Snicket

If you walk and read at the same time,
your book might end with a lamppost.

Contributing illustrators

Simini Blocker

Noelle Stevenson

Risa Rodil

Kiernan Sjursen-Lien

Karl James Mountford

Jonathan Burton

 Cynthia Lopez

Plakiat | Maks Bereski

 Isabel Talsma

 M. S. Corley

 Rachel Schweiger

Cynthia Lopez

Karl James Mountford

Ima Tri Kurniawati

Jay Cover

Albert Victoria

Lisa Cortes Bueno

Isabel Talsma

Anna Hoyle

Anna Hoyle

Nathanna Érica

Izzy Abreu

Olivia Huynh

Cynthia Lopez

Louis Kynd

Cynthia Lopez

Cynthia Lopez

Caeleigh Boara

M. S. Corley

Juan Osorno

Jonathan Burton

Cynthia Lopez

Teemu Juhani

Lara Mendes

Cynthia Lopez

Lara Mendes

Olivia Huynh

M. S. Corley

Martina Mastroieni

Cynthia Lopez

Hanna Wainio

Albert Victoria

Karl James Mountford

Olivia Huynh

Jay Cameron

Isabel Talsma

Aleesha Nandhra

Cynthia Lopez

Izzy Abreu

Jack Gallagher

Cynthia Lopez

M. S. Corley

Elizabeth Baddeley

Art of Gwencha

M. S. Corley

Laura Ellen Anderson

Cynthia Lopez

Isabel Talsma

Pierre Kleinhouse

Other published works

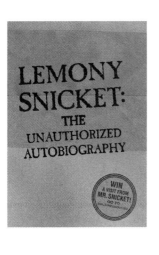

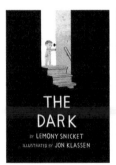

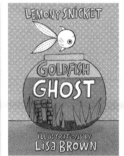

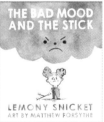

stock art

VectorPot (typewriter) / Shutterstock
Andrei Mayatnik (business card) / Shutterstock
lynea (clock) / Shutterstock
alya_haciyeva (acorn) / Shutterstock
Linor R (rain) / Shutterstock
Manekina Serafima (alligator) / Shutterstock
Lifestyle Graphic (book) / Shutterstock
rangizzz (newspaper) / Shutterstock
Andrey_Kuzmin (letter) / Shutterstock
Robyn Mackenzie (mirror) / Shutterstock
Vangelis_Vassalakis (crumbs) / Shutterstock
Olga Kostina (telephone) / Shutterstock
ChiccoDodiFC (black cloud) / Shutterstock
Lina Keil (broccoli) / Shutterstock
pio3 (globe) / Shutterstock
Martial Red (duck) / Shutterstock
Patty Chan (blackboard) / Shutterstock
Quang Ho (napkins) / Shutterstock
Kriang kan (lampost) / Shutterstock